A Tribute to
THE YOUNG AT HEART

VIRGINIA HAMILTON

By Jill C. Wheeler

Published by Abdo & Daughters, 4940 Viking Drive, Suite 622, Edina, Minnesota 55435.

Copyright © 1997 by Abdo Consulting Group, Inc., Pentagon Tower, P.O. Box 36036, Minneapolis, Minnesota 55435 USA. International copyrights reserved in all countries. No part of this book may be reproduced in any form without written permission from the publisher.

Printed in the United States.

Cover and Interior Photo credits: Scholastic
                              Harcourt Brace–Carlo Ontal

Special Thanks to Virginia Hamilton and Arnold Adoff

Edited by Lori Kinstad Pupeza

Library of Congress Cataloging-in-Publication Data

Wheeler, Jill., 1964-
        Virginia Hamilton / Jill C. Wheeler
            P.   cm. -- (Tribute to the young at heart)
        Includes Index.
        Summary: A biography of the children's writer known for her varied novels and interest in black history.

        ISBN 1-56239-790-7

        1. Hamilton, Virginia--juvenile literature. 2. Afro-America women authors--
        20th century--Biography--Juvenile Literature. 3. Children's stories--Authorship
        --Juvenile literature. [1. Hamilton, Virginia. 2. Authors, America. 3.
        Afro-Americans--Biography. 4. Women--Biography.] I. Title. II. Series.

        PS3558.A444Z95   1997
        813' .54--dc21   97-3790
                                                              CIP
                                                              AC

Table of Contents

SPIN ME A TALE

Young Virginia Hamilton curled her legs beneath her on the cozy rug by the furnace. In front of her, the local librarian opened a book. Silence fell over Virginia and the other children. The librarian began to tell a story.

Virginia listened to the librarian's stories at least once a week. Sometimes she went twice a week. She loved to lose herself in tales of far-away places and times past.

Stories always had been a big part of Virginia's life. She thought her mother's family told the best stories. Many were about Virginia's grandfather. His name was Levi Perry. He had been born a slave but had escaped. He traveled north on the Underground Railroad. He settled in southern Ohio to become a farmer.

The Underground Railroad fascinated young Virginia. She asked her aunts and uncles to tell her stories about it. As she grew, she learned it was not a real railroad at all. It was a network of people and places. All the people on the railroad wanted to help slaves escape slavery and live in freedom.

The network worked well. Few people who knew about it talked about it. Many people went to their graves never telling how they escaped. They knew if they talked, people in favor of slavery might destroy the network. They didn't want to ruin the chance for other slaves to escape, too.

Virginia never forgot those stories of the Underground Railroad. Years later, she featured it in a mystery novel she wrote. She called it *The House of Dies Drear*. It is about a family that moves into a huge old house. They learn the house once was part of the Underground Railroad. Its rooms are full of sliding panels and secret passages. Rumor has it a ghost haunts the house.

The hero of the book is a young man named Thomas. He and his father explore the house and find a secret treasure. *The House of Dies Drear* won The Edgar Allen Poe Award in 1969. The award recognizes outstanding mystery stories.

The Edgar Award is just one of many honors Virginia Hamilton has received for her work. Her career has spanned nearly thirty years. She's written more than 30 books and edited several others. Her work is full of originality, imagination, and depth. She is considered one of today's outstanding writers for children and young adults.

Virginia Hamilton.

BABY OF THE BUNCH

Virginia Esther Hamilton was born March 12, 1936, in Yellow Springs, Ohio. She was the fifth child of Kenneth James Hamilton and Etta Belle Perry Hamilton. As the baby of the family, she remembers that all the attention spoiled her. She also remembers feeling she was always an important family member.

Growing up on the rich farmland of southern Ohio was a joy for Virginia. Her mother's brothers and sisters also lived nearby. Virginia spent many days traveling between their farms. She loved to talk to them and listen to their stories. If she grew tired walking between farms, she'd lie down in a field and rest.

"I grew up within the warmth of loving aunts and uncles," she said. "All reluctant farmers but great storytellers. I remember the tales best of all. My father . . . was the finest of the storytellers. Mother, too, could take a slice of fiction floating around the family and polish it into a saga."

With so many brothers and sisters, Virginia thought she didn't have to do many chores. She often played with her cousin Marleen instead. Sometimes they picked berries and greens and sold them. They used the money to go to town and watch scary movies like *Frankenstein* or *The Wolfman*. Sometimes she and Marlene forgot they still had to walk home in the dark after the movie. They were more afraid than they had been in the theater!

Life in the Hamilton household was full and busy. Sometimes Virginia would go with her brother on his paper route. He pulled her on his sled as they slid through the Ohio winter. He told her his dreams. She said later that listening to his dreams helped her become a writer. "If you dream hard enough," he told her, "Your dreams will come true."

Virginia often would awake at night to the sound of her father playing his mandolin. "I remember I could wake at any hour before dawn and hear . . . his mandolin," she said. "The sound was a comfort because I never liked the night."

Kenneth Hamilton was a talented musician. He played in mandolin clubs around the nation. He dreamed of being a famous mandolin player. Sadly, he never could realize his dream. He was a black man and they could not join the musicians' union because of race prejudices. Non-union musicians could not play in the great concert halls. Kenneth played in small dance halls and on the radio instead.

BUDDING WRITER

Meanwhile, Virginia attended small country schools. There she learned some English and history. She was the only African-American girl in her class until seventh grade. She realized the teachers never said anything about Black history. Yet she wanted to know more.

It was in seventh grade that Virginia began to pay attention to her writing. She always had enjoyed writing. Now it became more important. She participated in many activities. She did the low hurdles in track. She was a cheerleader, too. Yet she always went back to reading and writing. She also dreamed of the day she could leave Yellow Springs.

The day Marlene got married was a sad one for Virginia. She realized she had lost her best friend. That night, she got a phone call from a teacher. The teacher had arranged for Virginia to receive a college scholarship! Virginia had never dreamed that she would be able to go to college. The news delighted her.

She began her studies at Antioch College in her hometown of Yellow Springs, Ohio. Fortunately, the college offered a major in writing. Virginia wrote a children's story while she was there. Years later it would become the basis for her first book, *Zeely*.

Later, at Ohio State University, one of her teachers encouraged Virginia to pursue her talent. "He told me that I really ought to leave school, go to New York, and try to become published," Virginia remembered. In the summer of 1955, she did just that.

Virginia as a young girl.

NEW YORK, NEW YORK

Virginia began spending her summers as a bookkeeper in New York City. She ended up moving there. "I don't have a clear recollection of the day I officially left home to go to New York," Virginia recalled. "My plan was to find a cheap apartment, a part-time job, write, and have a good time. And it all came together."

Virginia scheduled her job so she worked just four hours a day. The rest of the time she wrote, read, or spent time with other artists and writers. Virginia admits she didn't spend all her time working. "I worked hard at my writing, but wasn't singularly fixed on it," she said.

She sent some of her work to *The New Yorker* magazine. The magazine editors wrote back to her. They encouraged her and tried to help her improve her work. Still, it didn't work out. "I would never quite fit their mold," she said. "I was meeting all kinds of people and having a wonderful time. Seriousness came slowly."

While at a party in New York, Virginia met a poet named Arnold Adoff. They were married two years later on March 19, 1960. They took a wedding trip to Spain and northern Africa. Virginia couldn't forget about the trip. She loved African-American history and culture. She kept a cardfile for many years on Africa. The cardfile and her travels helped her write her first book, *Zeely*.

The book was an expansion of a short story Virginia wrote at Antioch College. A college friend of Virginia's remembered the story. That friend now worked at a publishing house. Virginia expanded the story into a novel at her friend's suggestion. She sent it to the publisher where her friend worked. The publisher agreed to produce the manuscript.

Zeely is about a girl called Geeder. One day Geeder sees a tall African-American woman tending pigs on a nearby farm. She imagines that the woman is a queen from an

African tribe. The woman finally convinces Geeder she's not a queen. Geeder learns to accept herself and others for what they are. That message helped *Zeely* earn a spot on the American Library Association's list of notable children's books in 1967.

Virginia wrote the final manuscript for *Zeely* when her daughter, Leigh, was young. She remembers how they went through the publishing process together. "We were together the whole time I worked on that book," she said. "I'd show her the typed pages and tell her what it was. I'd explain how I was sending it off, and when the galleys came back, we would look at them together. And then I'd send back the galleys and the proofs would come. Then, one day the book arrived with my name on the cover. Suddenly, it all came together for her. The look on her face was wonderful."

BACK TO THE COUNTRY

After 15 years in New York City, Virginia decided it was time to go home. "I loved the city until the moment I could no longer stand it," she said. "Which happened one day between four and five in the afternoon. I think what happened was that I had always found it too stimulating. No time to think. Only time to recoil or react."

Virginia, her husband and their children, Leigh and Jaime, moved back to Yellow Springs in 1969. They built a house on land that had been in Virginia's family for generations. Virginia settled down to write more books.

Her next project involved a subject she had always loved: the Underground Railroad. Yellow Springs had been a stop on the Underground Railroad. Many former slaves had settled in the area. Virginia had heard their stories as a child. She decided to weave them into a mystery novel for children. That was the beginning of *The House of Dies Drear.* The book later became a movie.

"*The House of Dies Drear* is one of my favorite books," Virginia said. "It is so full of all the things I love: excitement, mystery, black history, the strong, black family. In it I tried to pay back all those wonderful relatives who gave me so much in the past."

Virginia patterned the mansion in *The House of Dies Drear* on a real place she used to visit. She recalled she would shiver with fear when she walked by it. The book also features a hidden cave with a secret treasure. Yellow Springs has many limestone caves in the area.

Virginia also loves to dabble in science fiction and fantasy when she writes. Her next book was *The Time-Ago Tales of Jahdu.* The book is a collection of stories about little Jahdu, who was born in an oven. In the book, Mama Luka spins Jahdu stories out of thin air to entertain little James Edwards. Mama Luka is caring for James while his parents are at work. James learns about himself through the Jahdu stories.

Virginia wrote four books about Jahdu and his adventures. The stories are much like traditional folk tales. They involve such creatures as Sweetdream, Nightmare, and Trouble. Yet they also let readers connect with real life. For example, little Jahdu finds his greatest happiness when he becomes part of an African-American family in Harlem. Harlem is an area in New York City.

New York City also became the setting for her next book, *The Planet of Junior Brown*. Junior Brown is a 262-pound musical prodigy. Most people can't see beyond his weight. Yet Junior finds two friends. They meet with him in a secret room in the school basement. He learns that he can't live life on his own planet. He needs other people.

The American Library Association gave *The Planet of Junior Brown* a John Newbery Honor Book Award. The book also became a National Book Award finalist.

DOUBLE HONORS

Virginia's next novel came from a strange image that occurred to her one day. She saw in her mind's eye a young person running through the woods with lettuce leaves attached to his wrists. She thought about the image a lot. Then she turned it into a novel for children. The novel is *M.C. Higgins, the Great.*

The novel is about the Higgins family. The family has lived on Sarah's Mountain ever since M.C.'s great-grandmother, Sarah, escaped from slavery and settled there. Problems arise when people begin strip mining on the mountain. The mining creates a slag heap that threatens the Higgins home. M.C. spends many hours sitting on top of a tall pole looking at his mountain. He knows he must find a way to save his mountain and his home.

At first, Virginia thought no one would like M.C. Higgins. She spent nine months reworking it. The extra work was worth it. *M.C. Higgins, the Great* was the first book in history to win both the National Book Award and the Newbery Medal. It also won The Boston Globe Hour Book Award.

The book is not a happily-ever-after story. A critic in *The New York Times Book Review* said this instead. "It is warm, humane, and hopeful and does what every book should do. It creates characters with whom we can identify and for whom we care."

M.C. Higgins, the Great features a special place in Yellow Springs called Glen Healen. A glen is a narrow valley. Virginia often explored Glen Healen as a child, as did her brothers. Some of her other books feature the Ohio fields she played in as a child. Virginia uses these familiar landscapes to help her tales spring to life.

TACKLING TOUGH ISSUES

Virginia takes on the issue of interracial dating in one of her more recent books. *A White Romance* is about two interracial couples. Virginia looked to her son, Jaime, for help in writing the book. One important part of the book takes place at a rock concert.

"My son, a musician, was an invaluable help to me," she said. "He spent long hours talking with me into a tape recorder. He gave me the lingo, the sounds, the scents. All the hidden things you have to know. Because Jaime is such a marvelous storyteller, place . . . has a central role in *A White Romance*."

Virginia had to make some cuts in the manuscript before it was published. Her editors thought she was too graphic in some scenes between the young couples. However, her rock concert scene stayed the same.

FOCUS ON BLACK HISTORY

Virginia has used her interest in and knowledge of African-American culture to write nonfiction as well. "I have consistently written nonfiction, as well as fiction," Virginia said. "The nonfiction not only provides a rest from novels and stories, but satisfies a need to do ongoing research and tell the . . . stories of our people."

In 1975, she published a biography of Paul Robeson. Robeson was the son of a former slave. He became an internationally known singer and actor. The book took years to research and write. Virginia worked especially hard at it. She wanted readers to feel like they were walking hand in hand with Robeson as they learned about his life.

Virginia also edited an anthology of pieces about W.E.B. Du Bois. Du Bois edited a magazine called *Crisis*. The magazine was the publication of the National Association for the Advancement of Colored People (NAACP). Virginia had a special interest in Du Bois because her father had known him.

Virginia also wrote a book entitled *The People Could Fly*. The book is a collection of American black folk tales. It is an important book to Virginia.

"The slaves . . . had no power, no weapons to aid them in overcoming their oppressors," she said. "They used the folklore they created to comment on their lives . . . and give themselves comfort and strength."

Virginia wanted more than simply to share the folk tales with readers. She wanted readers to feel what it had been like to hear them. "There was no safe place where . . . slaves could sit down and simply tell stories except in the safety of the forests," she said. "They gathered under the cover of darkness to . . . discuss what was beyond the forest. Their meetings were so secret they dared not use their own names."

Another book, *Many Thousand Gone: African Americans from Slavery to Freedom* is a history book. It tells a part of the story of African Americans in the United States. It begins with the start of slavery and ends after the American Civil War. The book features the stories of individual slaves. The stories let readers see what it was like for black people during those years.

THE AUTHOR AT WORK

The M.C. Higgins image of the child and lettuce leaves is an example of one of the ways Virginia begins her books. "I work on a book in two ways," she said. "One day, there appears out of nowhere a small visual piece. A glimpse, say, of a small child struggling to put on rubber galoshes. At once the image disappears around a corner of my mind. I have to chase after it to see where it's going. I may not discover another image like it for some time."

"By then I've been at the typewriter for hours. I've explained why the child is putting on galoshes. That the hour is the middle of the night. That she needs the galoshes to get through heavy snow to find her dad. That she hears her dad singing while he sleds down a nearby hill. That her need for her father is greater than her fear of the cold, dark outside. By that time, I'm into the book."

"In another instance, there is a whole story in the dreams and fears of one character. That character appears in the mind completely realized. What becomes difficult is following this figure about as he gathers his neighbors, friends, and family . . . . Whether the story begins as a glimpse or as a whole idea, there is room within the novel for exploration in time, place and mind, and for change and growth."

Virginia usually writes about African-American characters. She says she does not do it on purpose. "When I decide to write a story, I don't say to myself, now I'm going to write a Black story. But it happens that I know Black people better than any other people because I am one of them."

"I grew up knowing what it is we are about. I am at ease with being Black. More than anything, I write about emotions, which are part of all people. But the constant is that the characters are Black, whether the story is fantasy or realism."

"Black folk tales, I believe, allow us to share in the known, the remembered, and the imagined together as Americans sharing the same history . . . . From teller to reader is the unbroken circle of communication. We are all together. That is what language does for us."

Virginia Hamilton
at her typewriter.

A LITERARY LEGACY

Critics agree Virginia's books present a challenge to readers. Her writing style is often complex. Her characters have many levels. It's not uncommon to find new meanings in her books each time you read them. The critics agree it is worthwhile to read her work.

Today, Virginia still lives with her family in southern Ohio. Her two children are grown and pursuing their own careers. Meanwhile, she continues to write about African-American people and experiences. She believes her books are useful for readers of all races.

"Books can, and do help us to live," she said. "Some may even change our lives."

"It's my hope never to be bored writing and never to bore children reading what I've written," she added.
With an imagination like Virginia's, it's unlikely she will be bored. And with her rich, vivid tales, it's unlikely her readers will be, either.

Some of Virginia Hamilton's books.

WRITINGS

Following is a list of books by Virginia Hamilton. Hamilton's books are worth the extra work needed to read them.

Zeely, Macmillan, 1967

The House of Dies Drear, Macmillan, 1968

The Time-Ago Tales of Jahdu, Macmillan, 1969

The Planet of Junior Brown, Macmillan, 1971

Time-Ago Lost: More Tales of Jahdu, Macmillan, 1973

M.C. Higgins, the Great, Macmillan, 1974

Paul Robeson: The Life and Times of a Free Black Man,
    Harper, 1974

Arilla Sun Down, Greenwillow, 1976

Justice and Her Brothers, Greenwillow, 1978

Jahdu, Greenwillow, 1980

Dustland, Greenwillow, 1980

The Gathering, Greenwillow, 1981

Sweet Whispers, Brother Rush, Philomel, 1982

The Magical Adventures of Pretty Pearl, Harper, 1983

Willie Bea and the Time the Martians Landed,
    Greenwillow, 1983

A Little Love, Philomel, 1984

Junius over Far, Harper, 1985

The People Could Fly: American Black Folktales, Knopf, 1985

*The Mystery of Drear House: The Conclusion of the Dies
     Drear Chronicle*, Greenwillow, 1987

A White Romance, Philomel, 1987

In the Beginning: Creation Stories from around the World,
     Harcourt, 1988

*Anthony Burns: The Defeat and Triumph of a Fugitive
     Slave*, Knopf, 1988

Bells of Christmas, Harcourt, 1989

The Dark Way: Stories from the Spirit World, Harcourt, 1990

Cousins, Putnam, 1990

The All Jahdu Storybook, Harcourt, 1991

*Many Thousand Gone: African-Americans from Slavery to
     Freedom*, Knopf, 1992

Drylongso, Harcourt, 1992

Plain City, Scholastic, 1993

Her Stories, Scholastic, 1995

Jaguarundi, Scholastic, 1995

When Birds Could Talk And Bats Could Sing, Scholastic, 1996

GLOSSARY OF TERMS

Galley — A sample of what a printed page will look like.

Galoshes — Rubber boots worn over shoes to protect them.

Glen — A narrow valley.

Interracial — Involving people of different races.

Lingo — Language unique to a particular interest.

Major — A field of study in college.

Mandolin — A stringed musical instrument.

Oppressors — People who unjustly hurt or have control over other people.

Prodigy — A very talented child.

Proof — A sample of what a printed page will look like.

Recoil — To draw back from something.

Reluctant — Unwilling.

Saga — A long tale.

Slag — The waste left over after mining operations.

Strip Mining — Taking ores from the surface of the land.

Underground Railroad — A network of people and places used to help slaves escape to freedom.

Union — A group of workers who band together for better working conditions.

INDEX